Draw A Magical Fairy World – Beginner Lessons Book

Learn How to Illustrate a Fairy Book Like a True Disney Artist

Fairy Book

By : Gala Publication

2

Published By :

Gala Publication

© Copyright 2015 – Gala Publication

ISBN-13: **978-1522708834**
ISBN-10: **1522708839**

Table of Contents

ANIME FAIRY

STEP 1

STEP 2

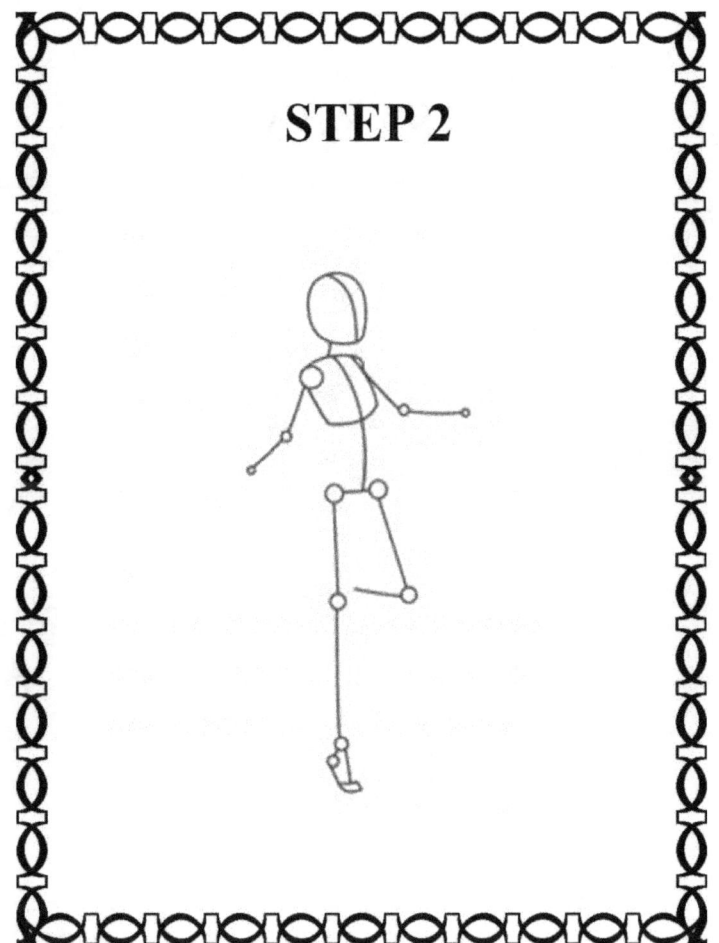

STEP 3

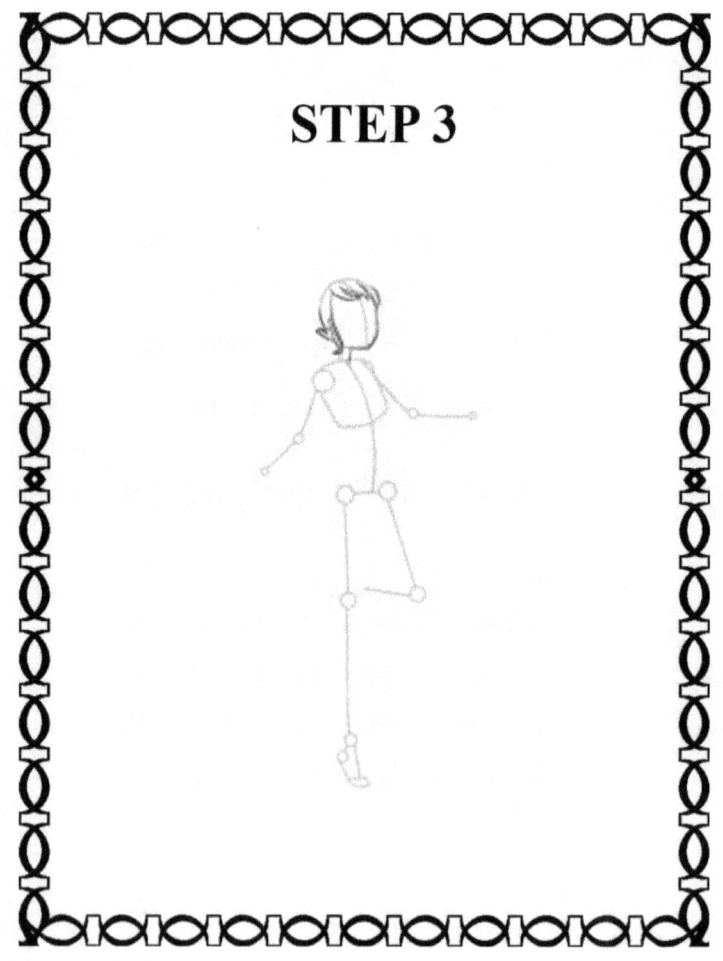

STEP 4

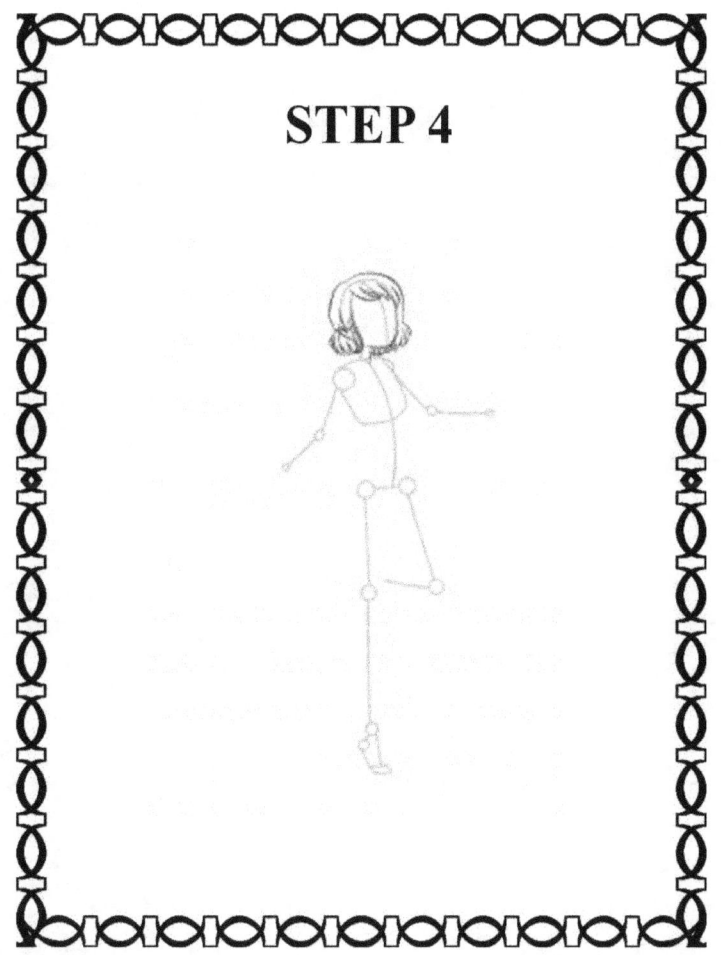

STEP 5

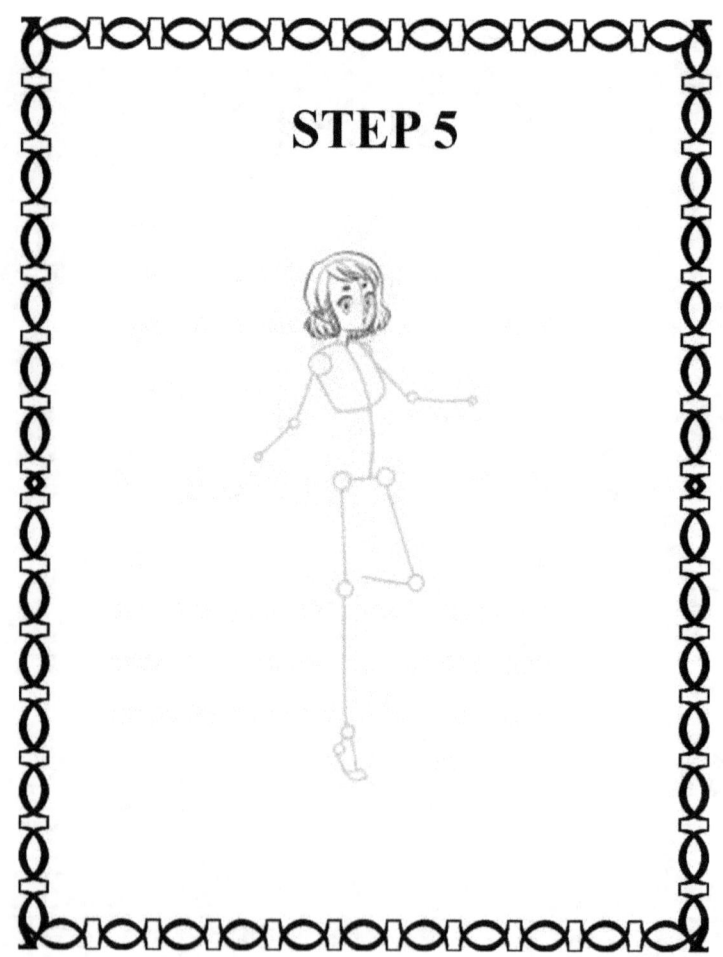

STEP 6

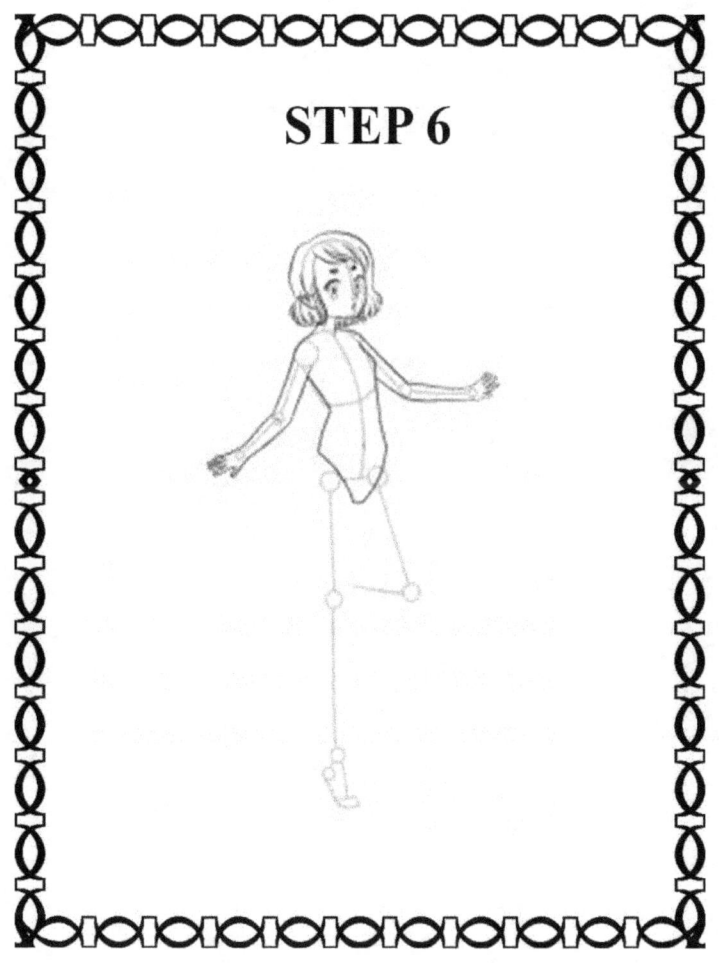

STEP 7

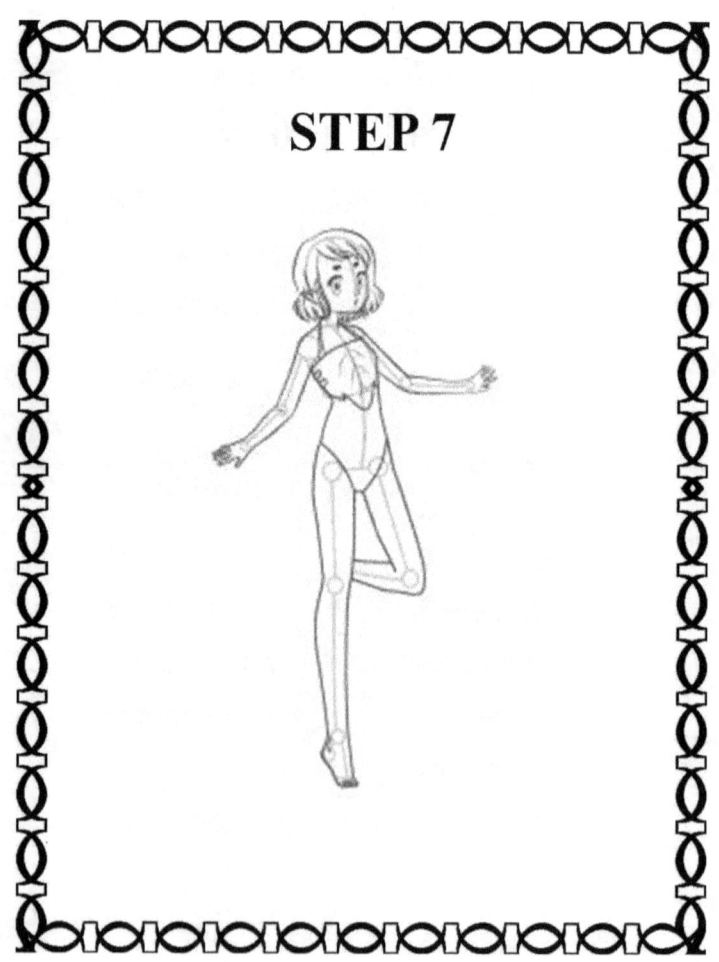

STEP 8

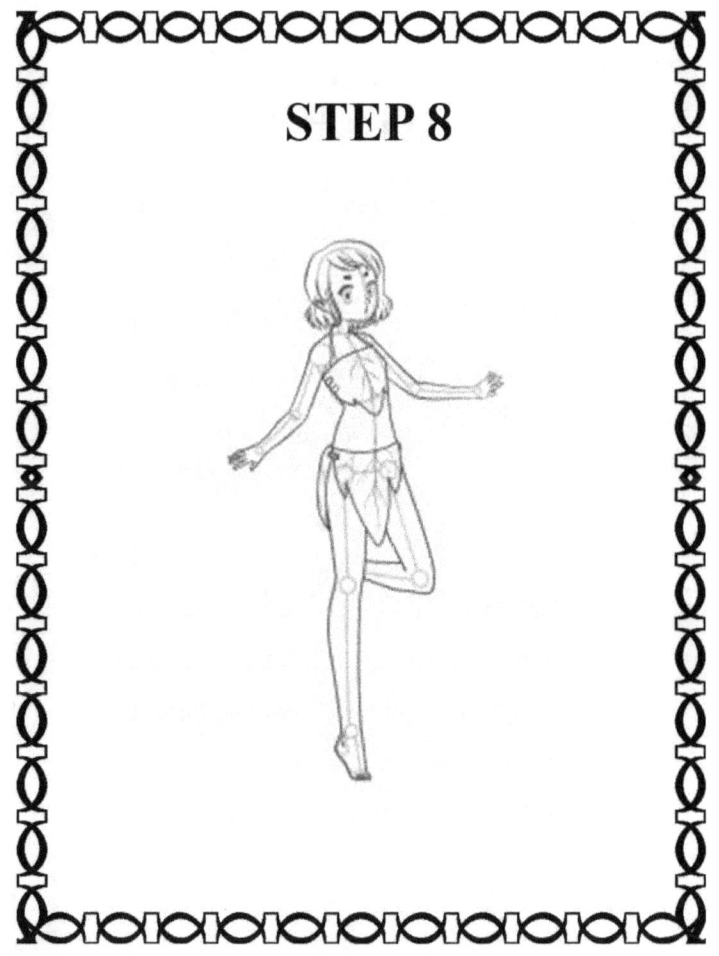

STEP 9

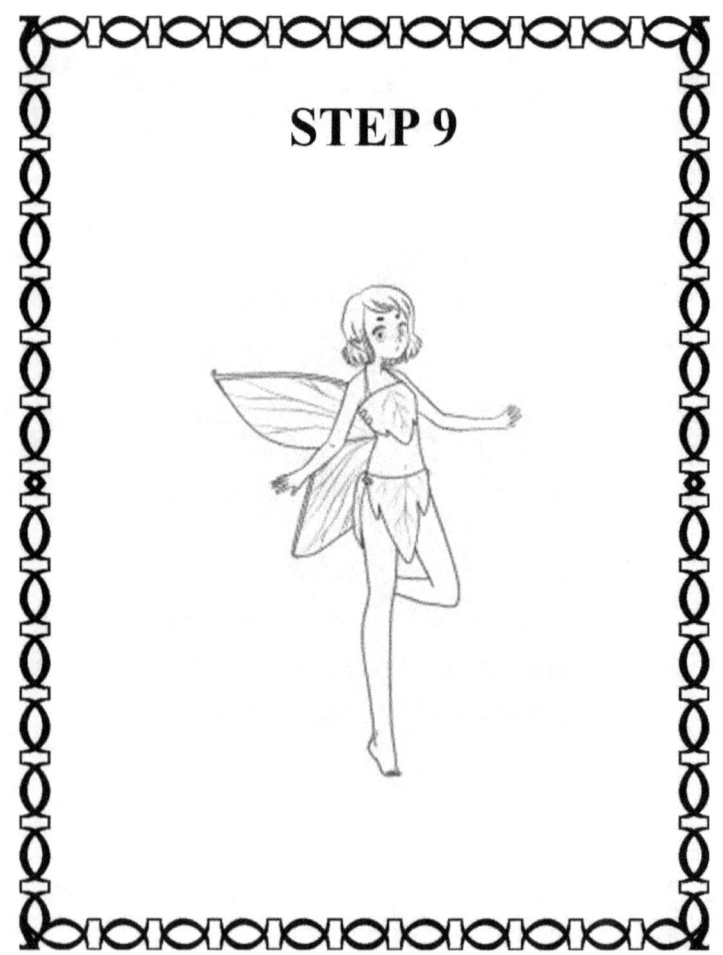

STEP 10

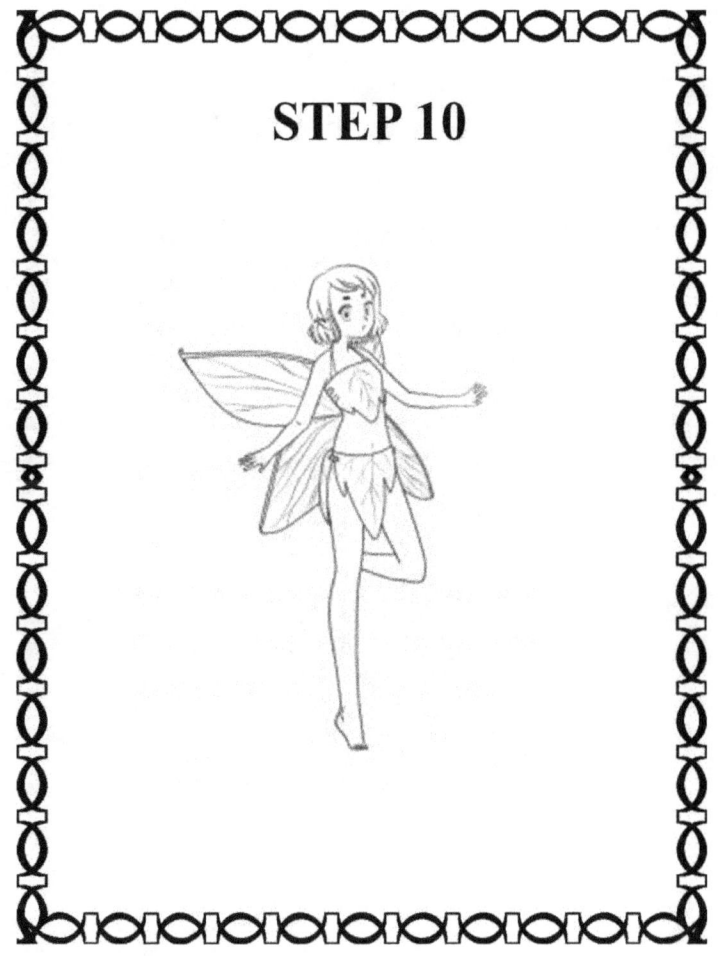

CUTE FAIRY

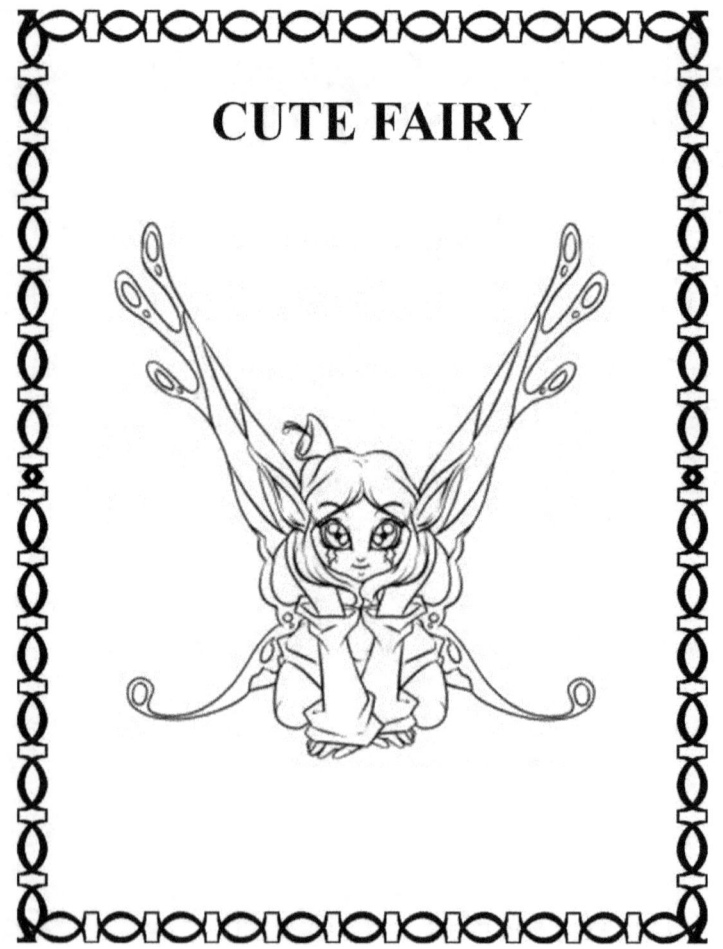

STEP 1

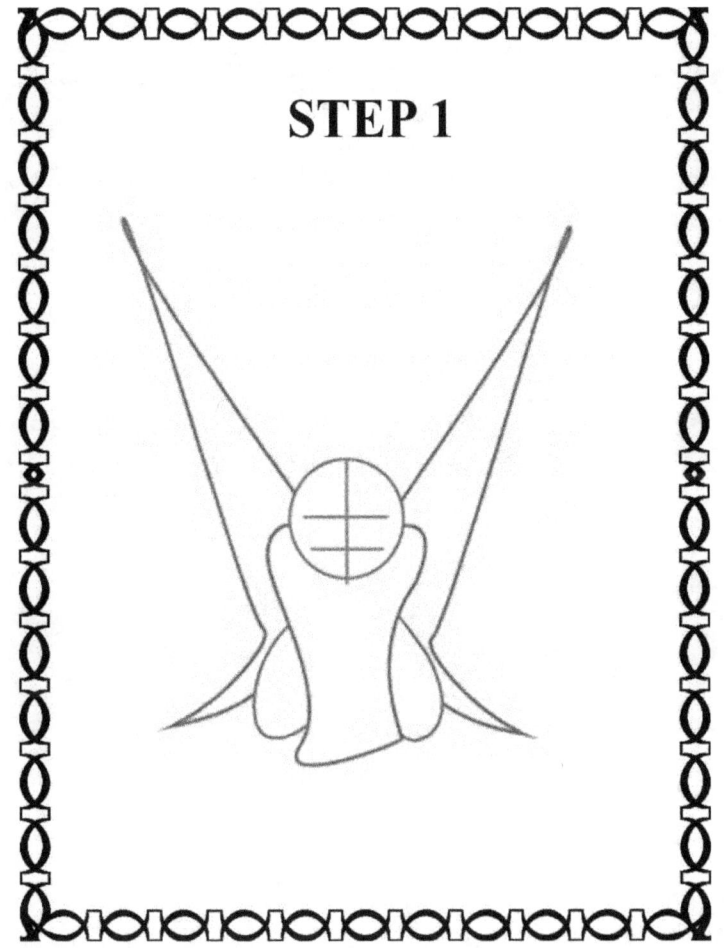

STEP 2

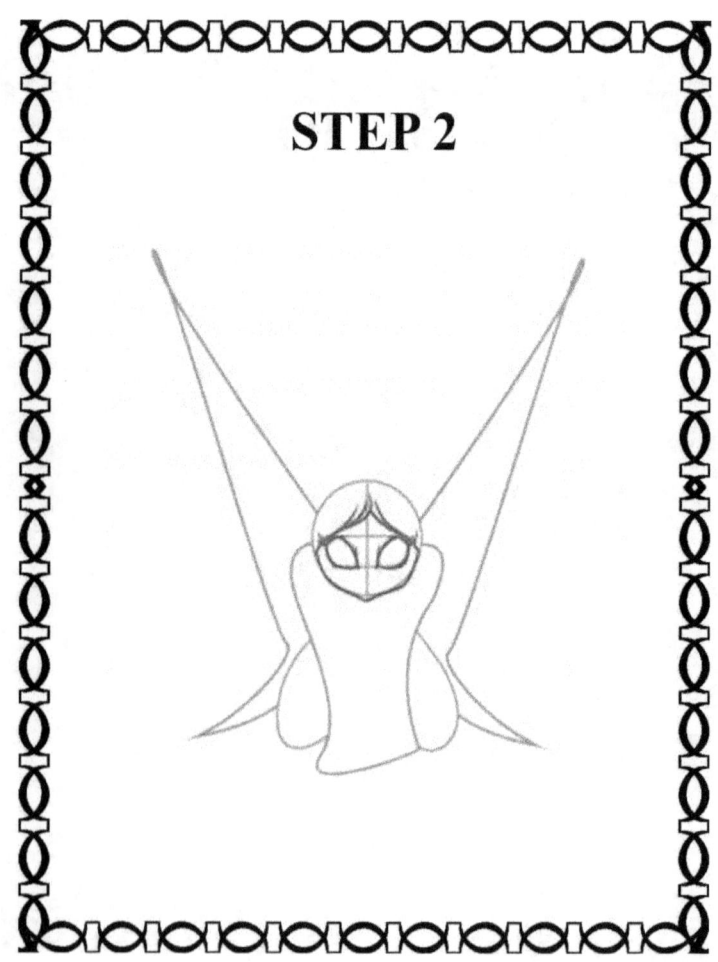

STEP 3

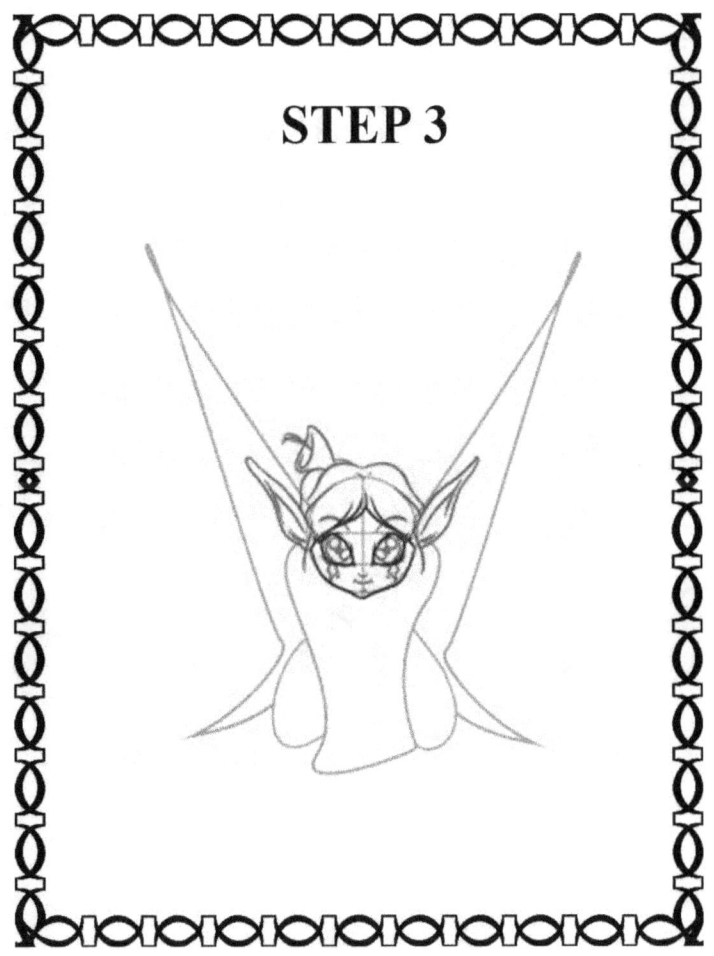

STEP 4

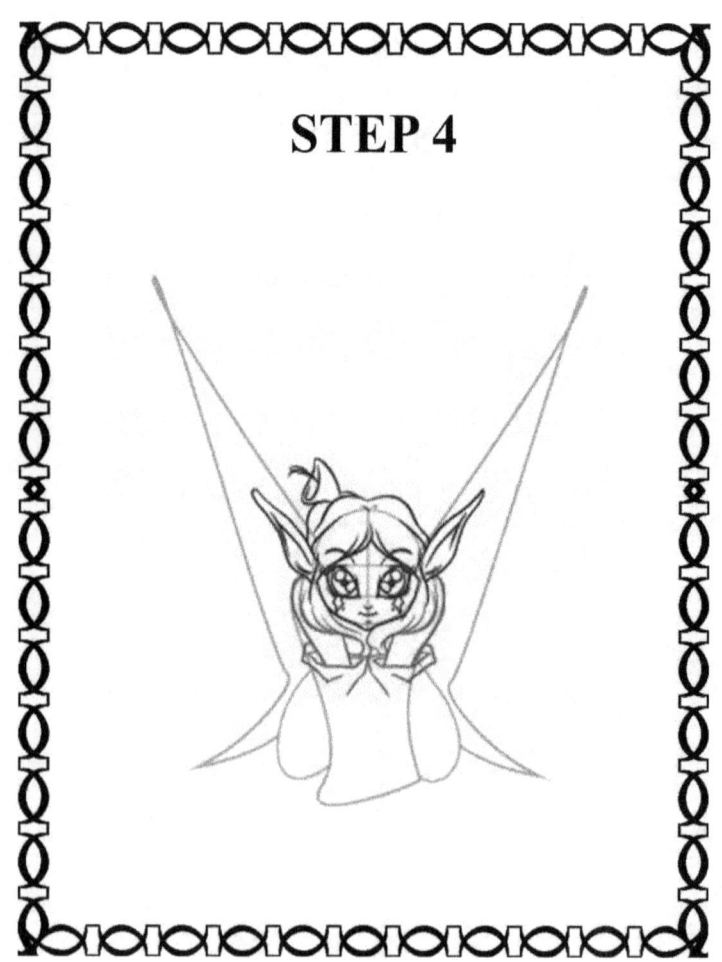

STEP 5

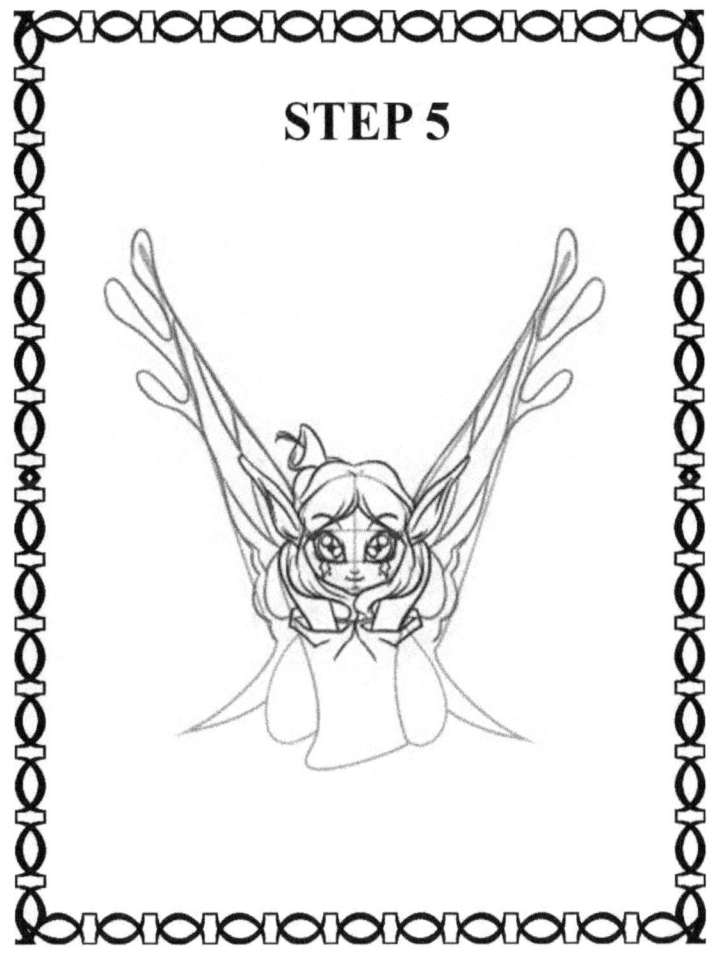

STEP 6

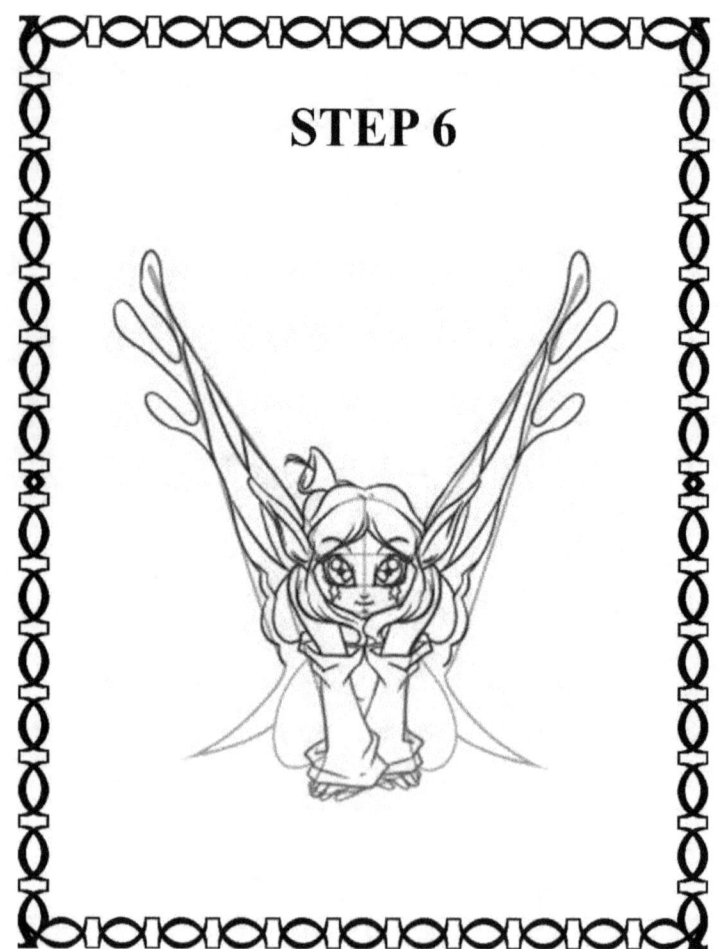

STEP 7

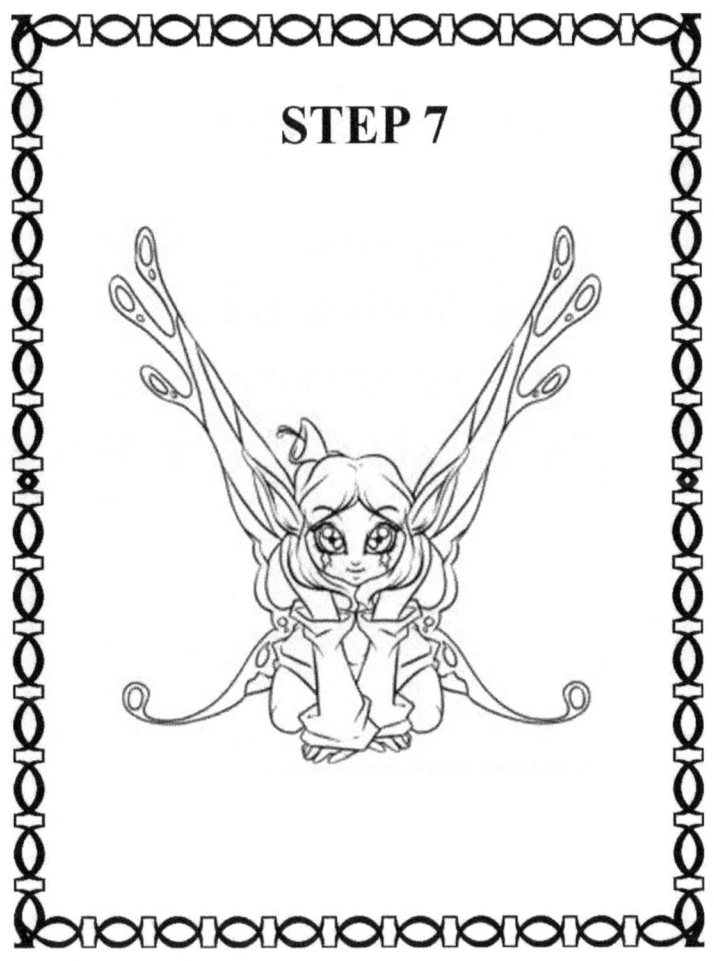

FLOWER FAIRY

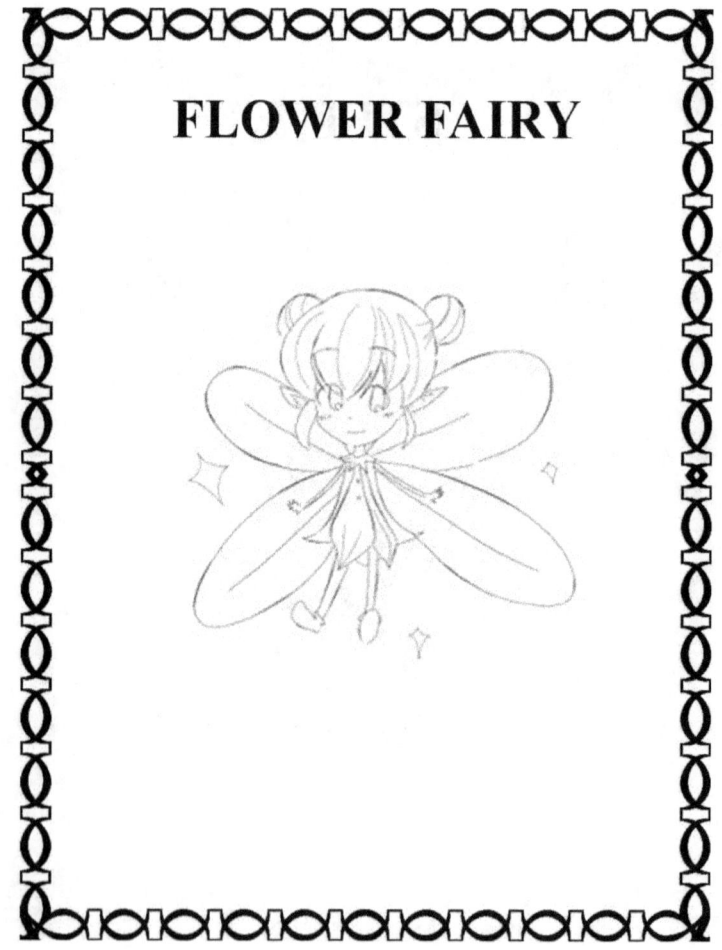

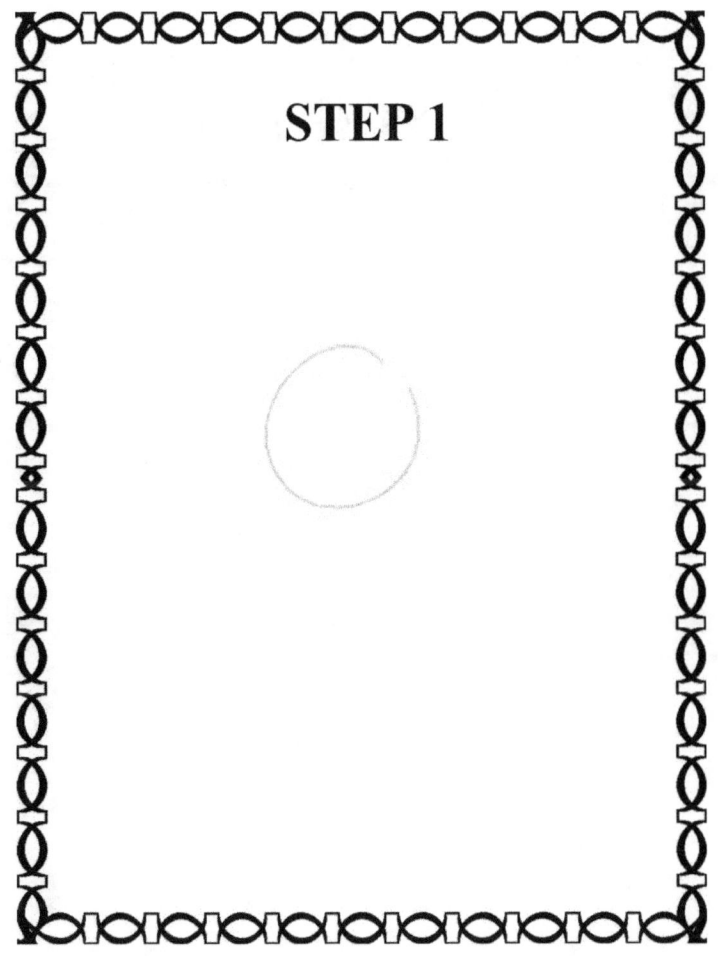

STEP 1

STEP 2

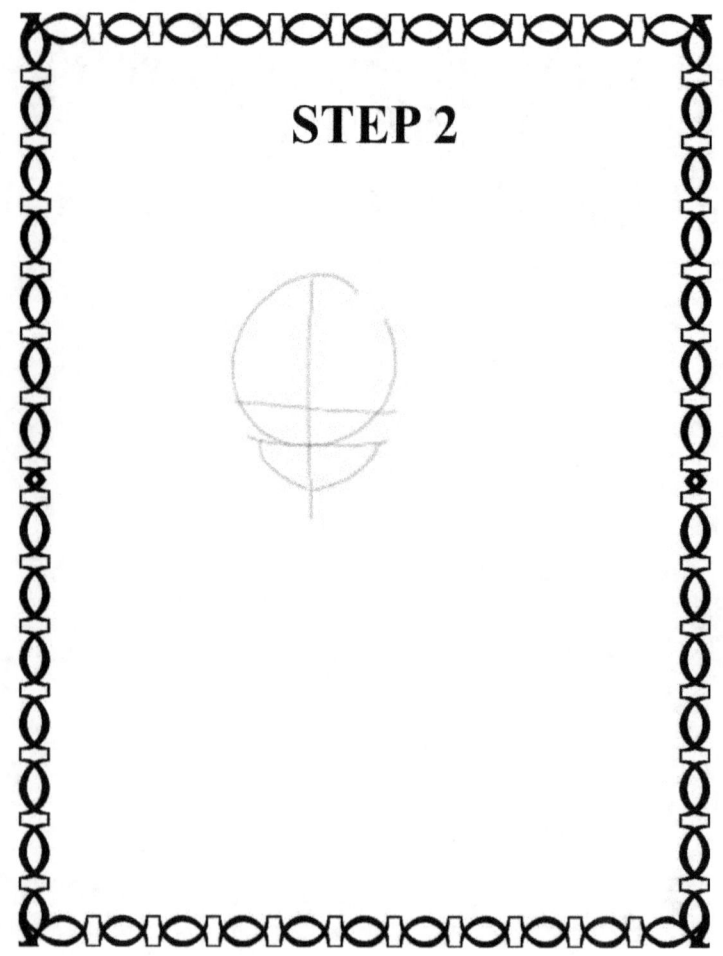

STEP 3

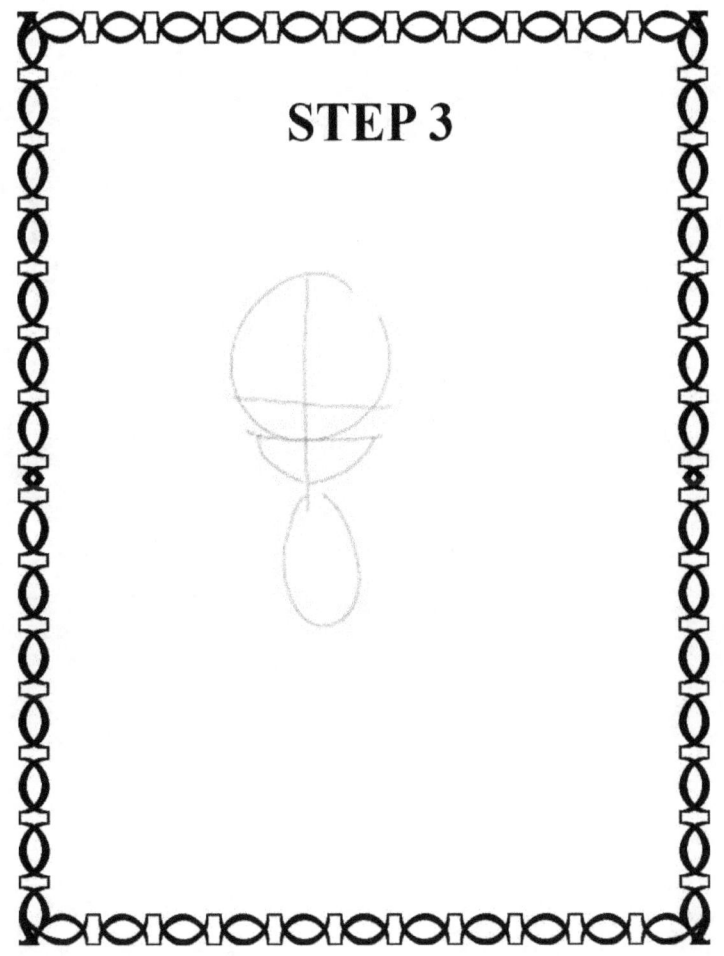

STEP 4

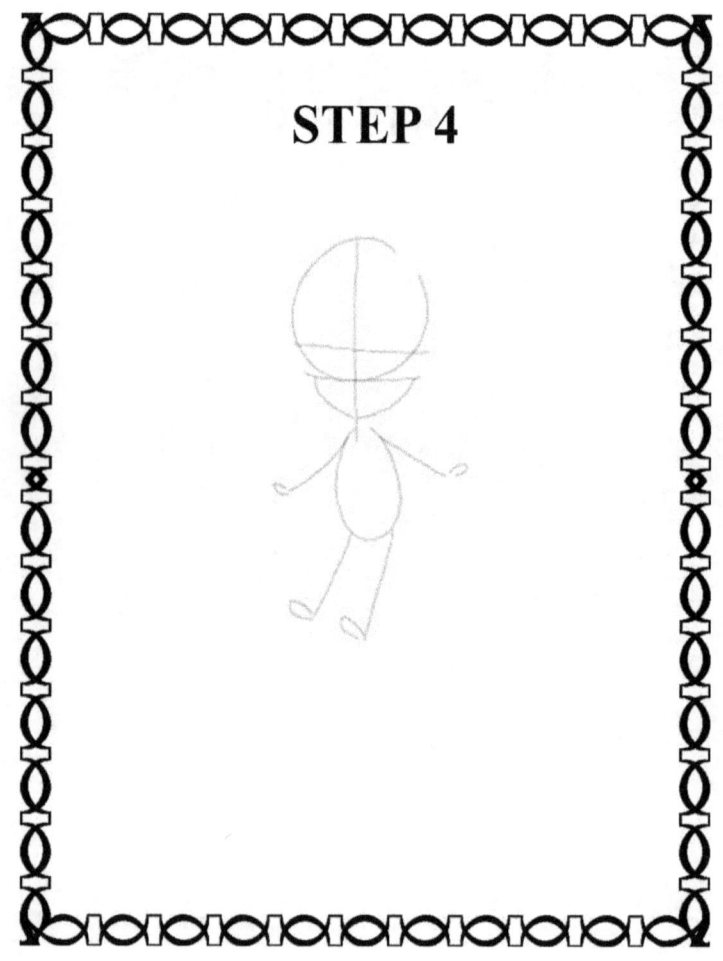

STEP 5

STEP 6

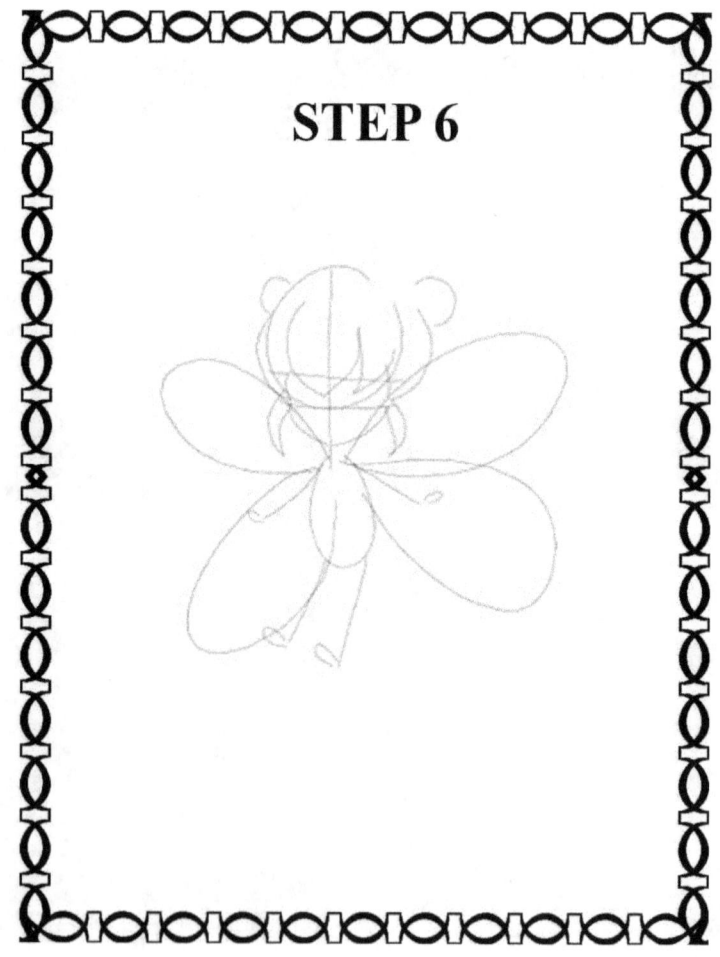

STEP 7

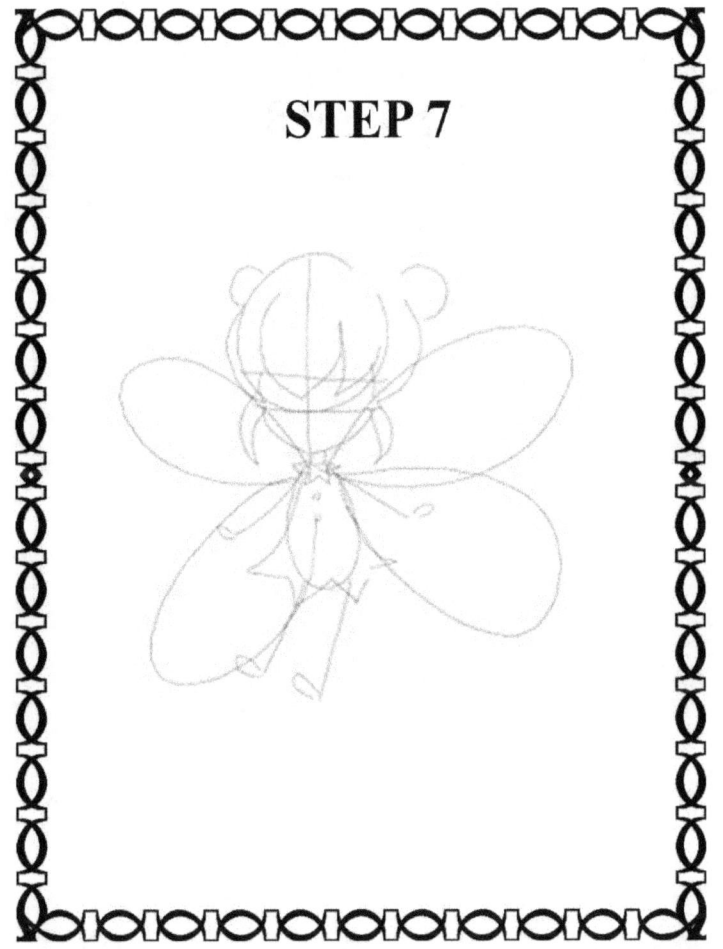

STEP 8

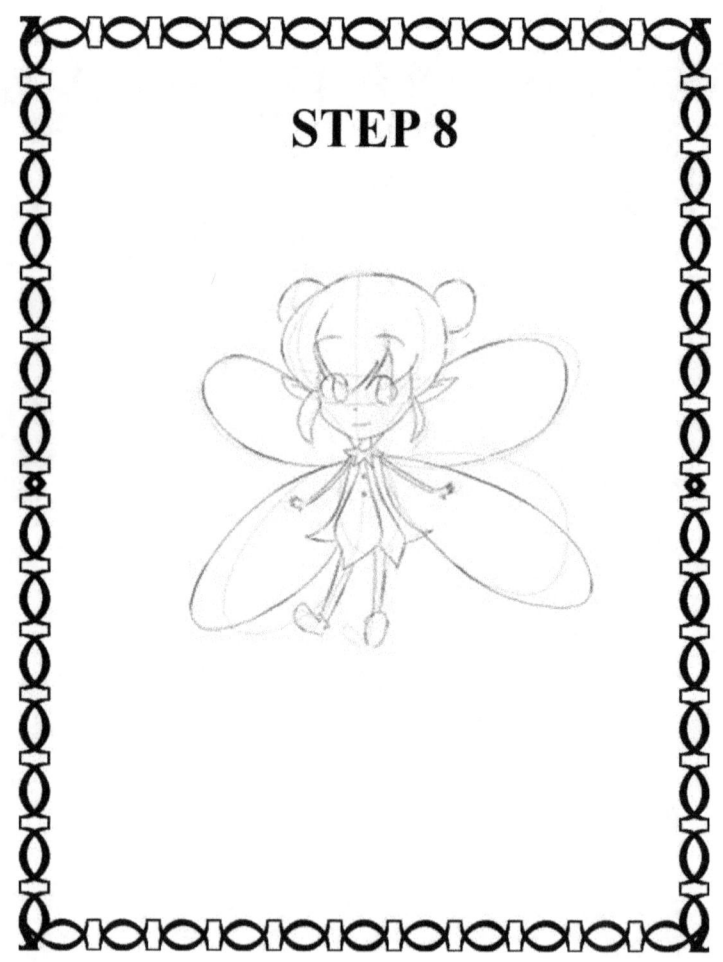

STEP 9

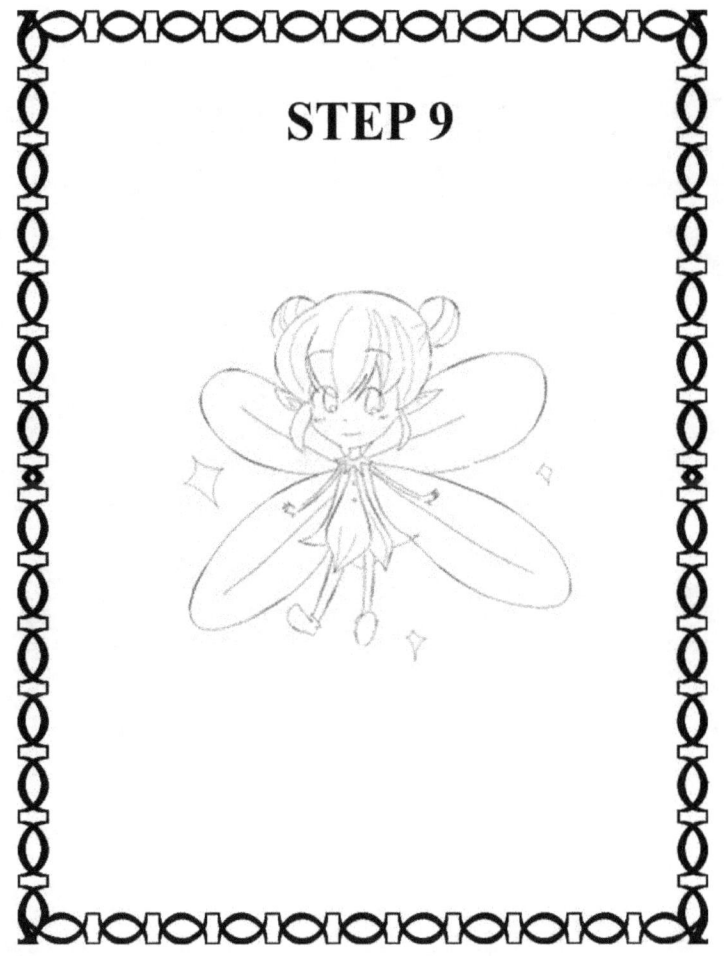

HELL FAIRY

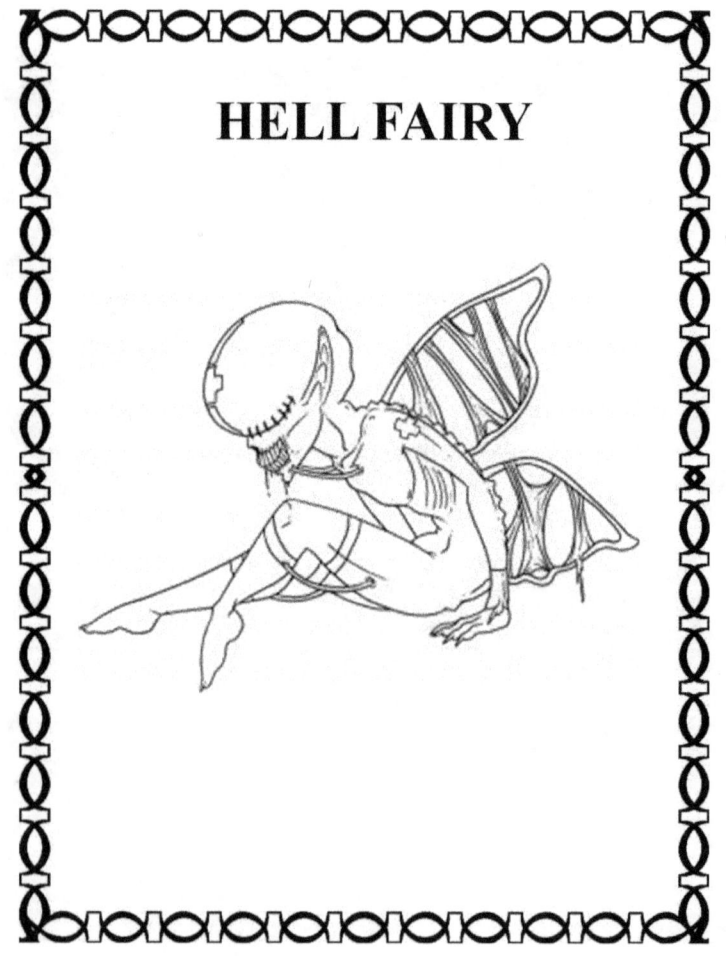

STEP 1

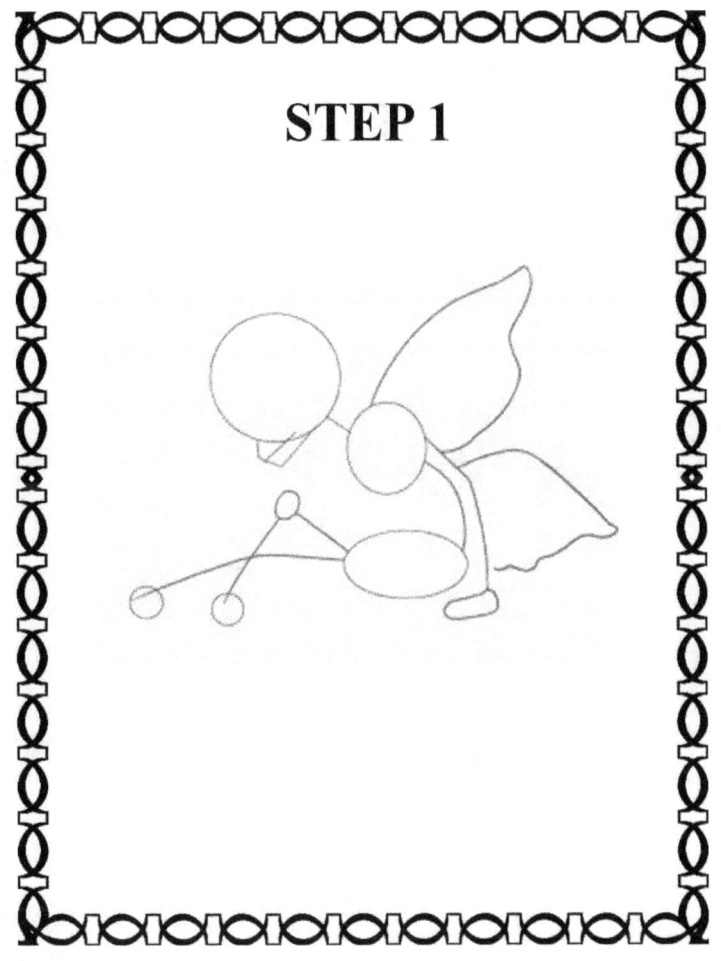

STEP 2

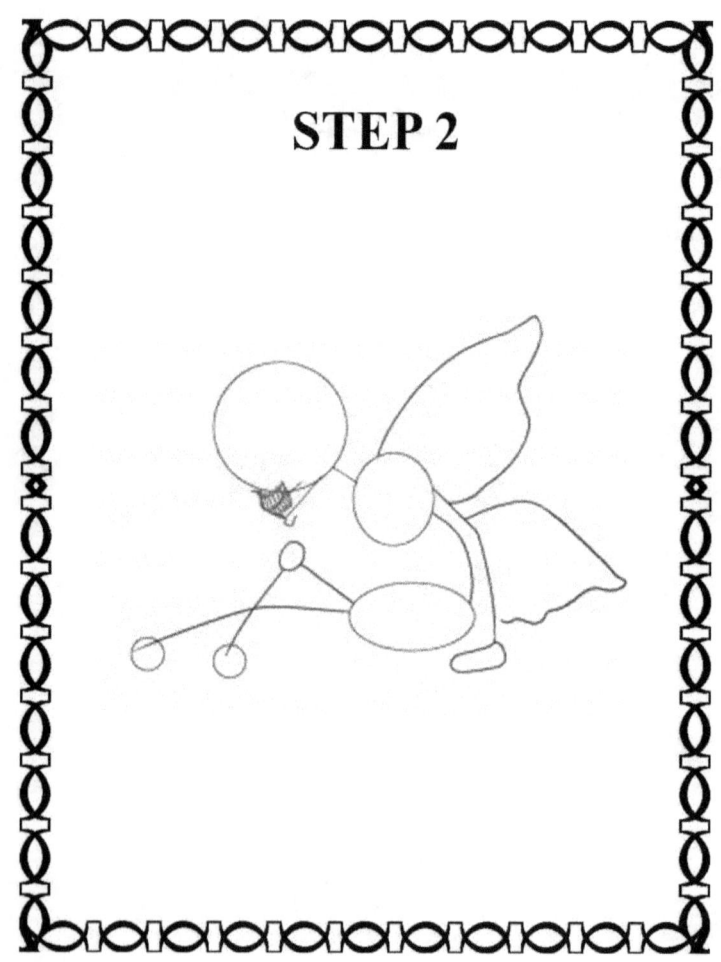

STEP 3

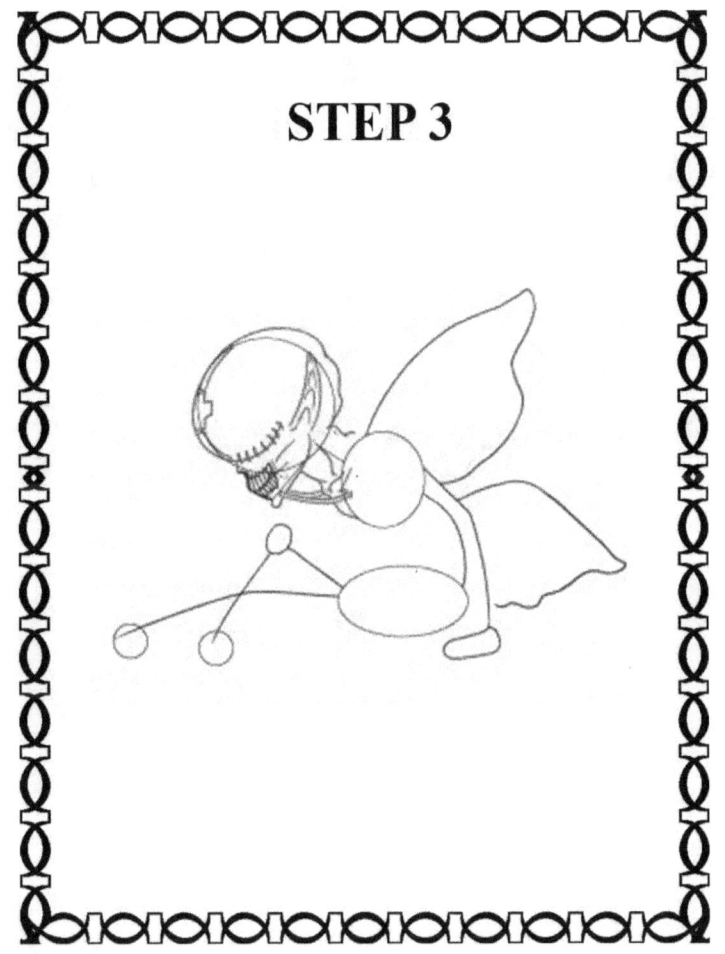

STEP 4

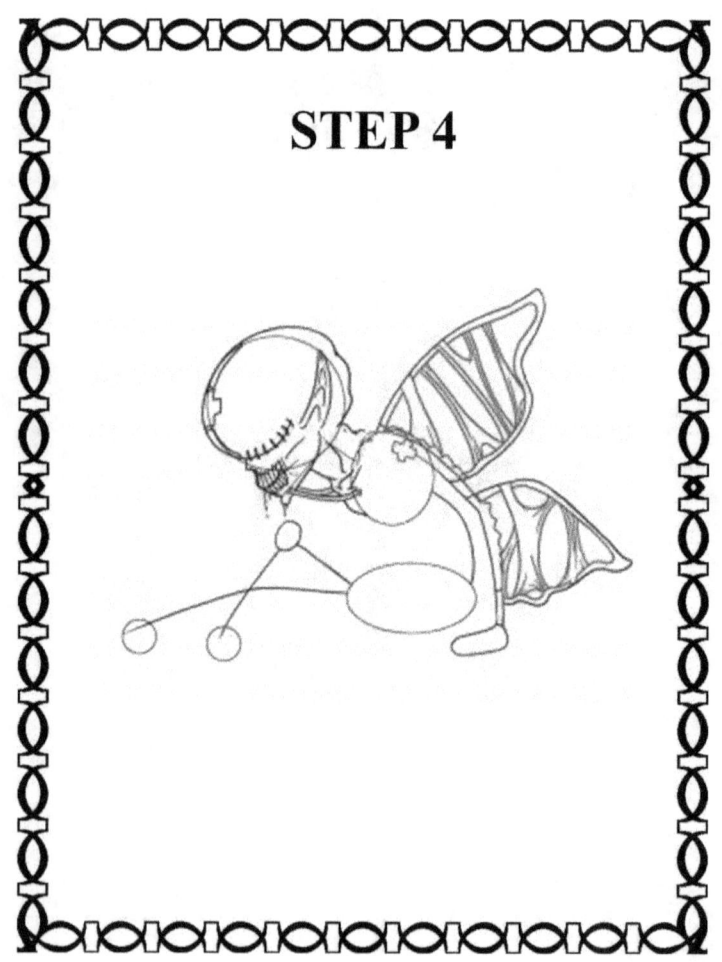

STEP 5

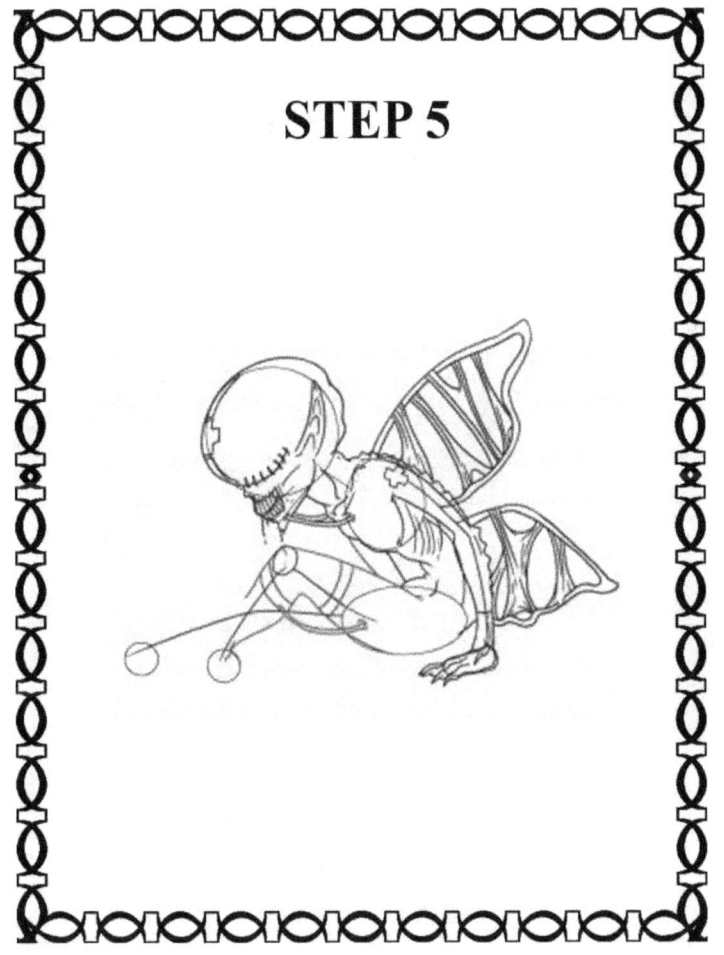

STEP 6

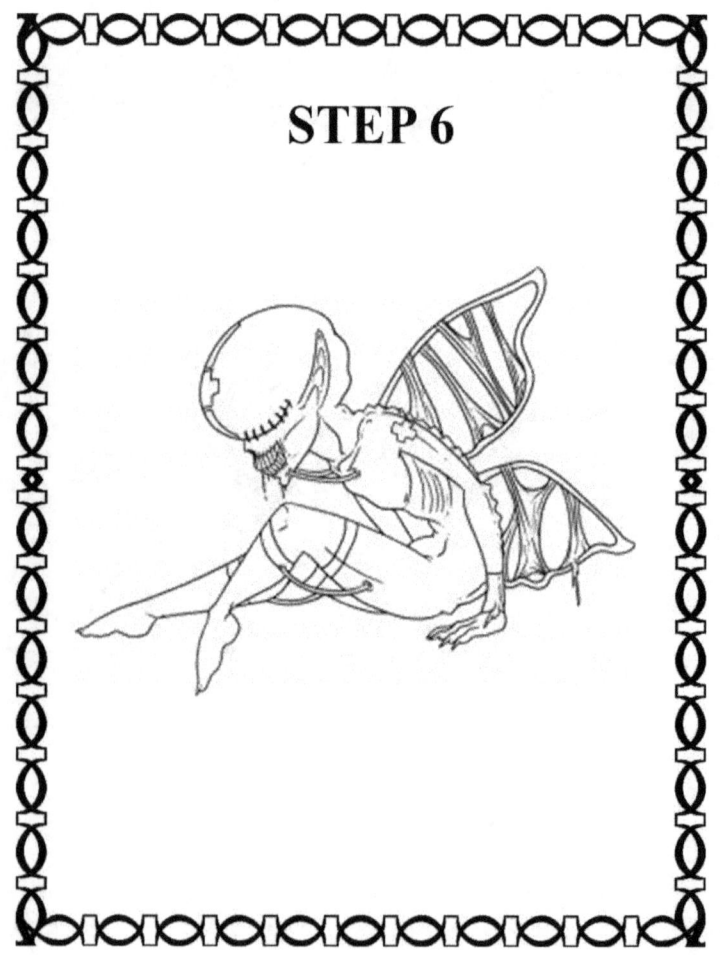

SIMPLE FAIRY

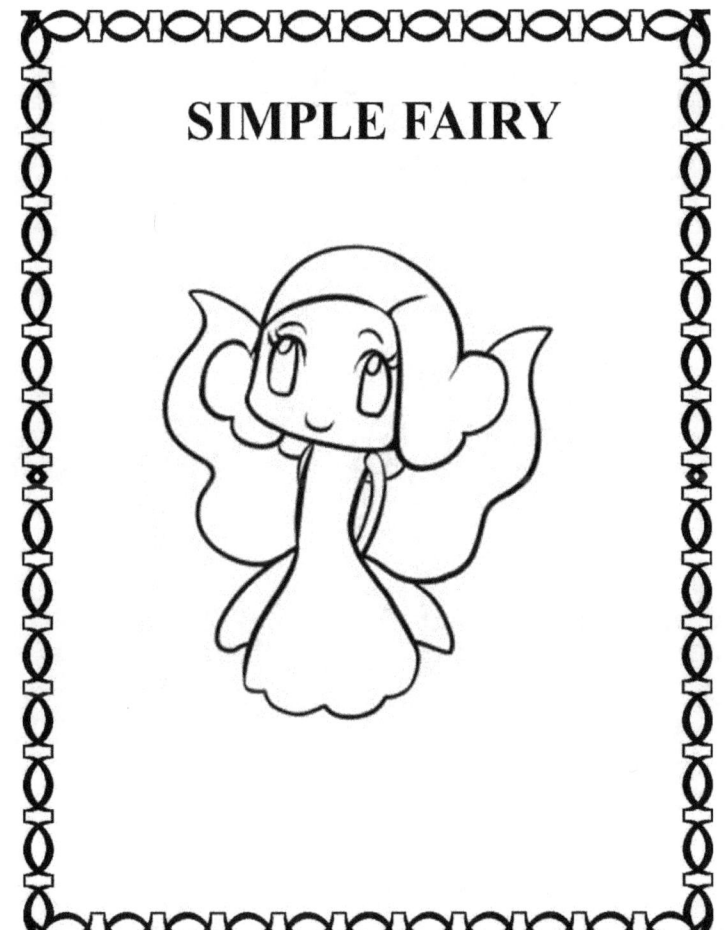

STEP 1

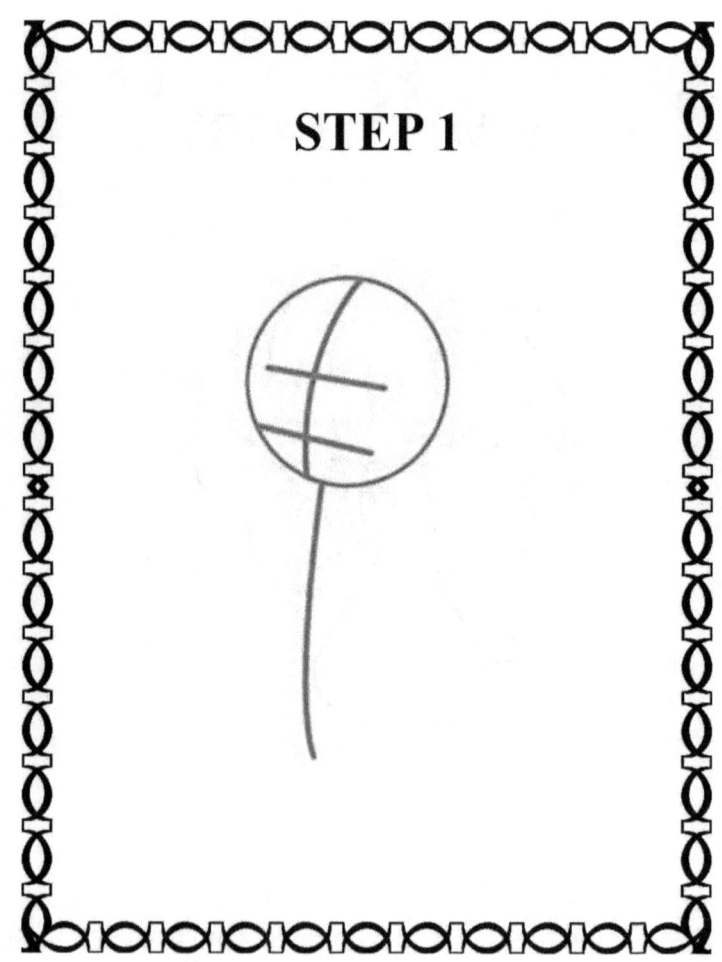

STEP 2

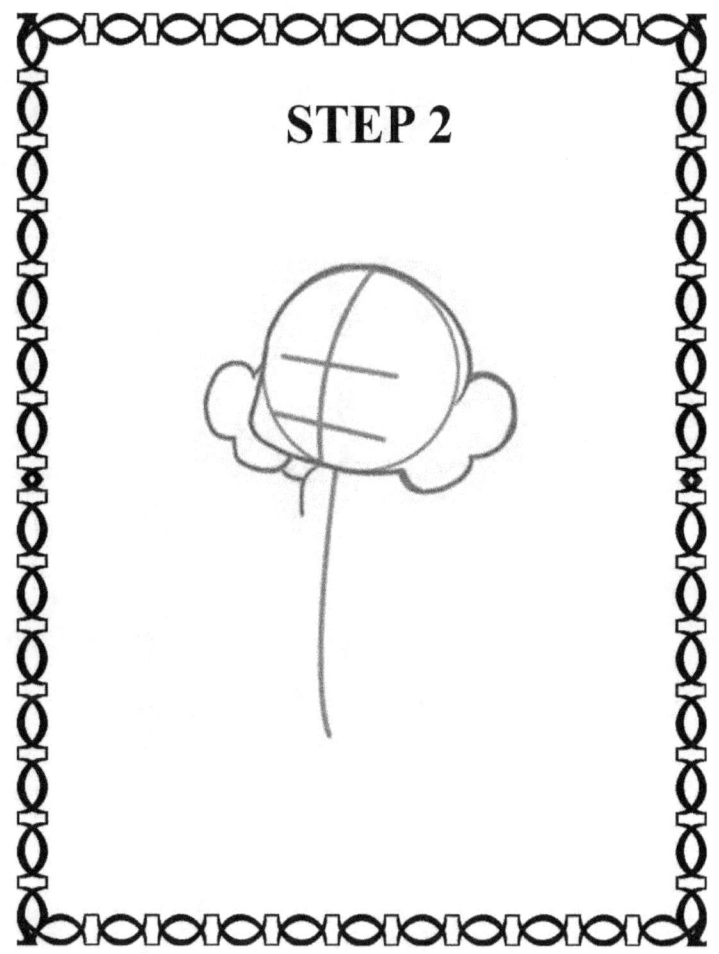

STEP 3

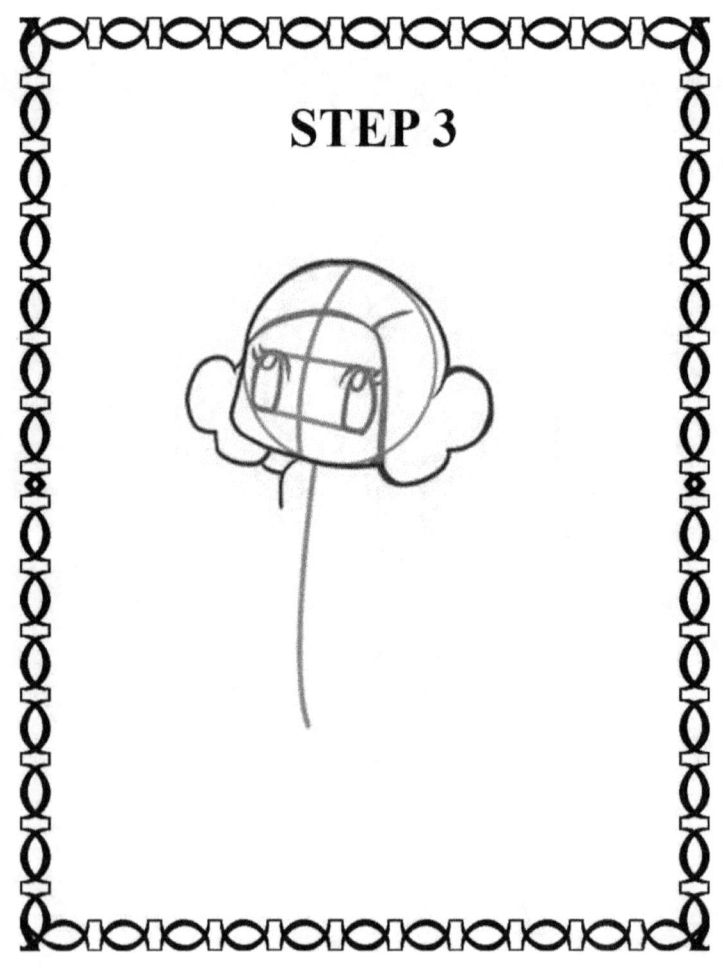

STEP 4

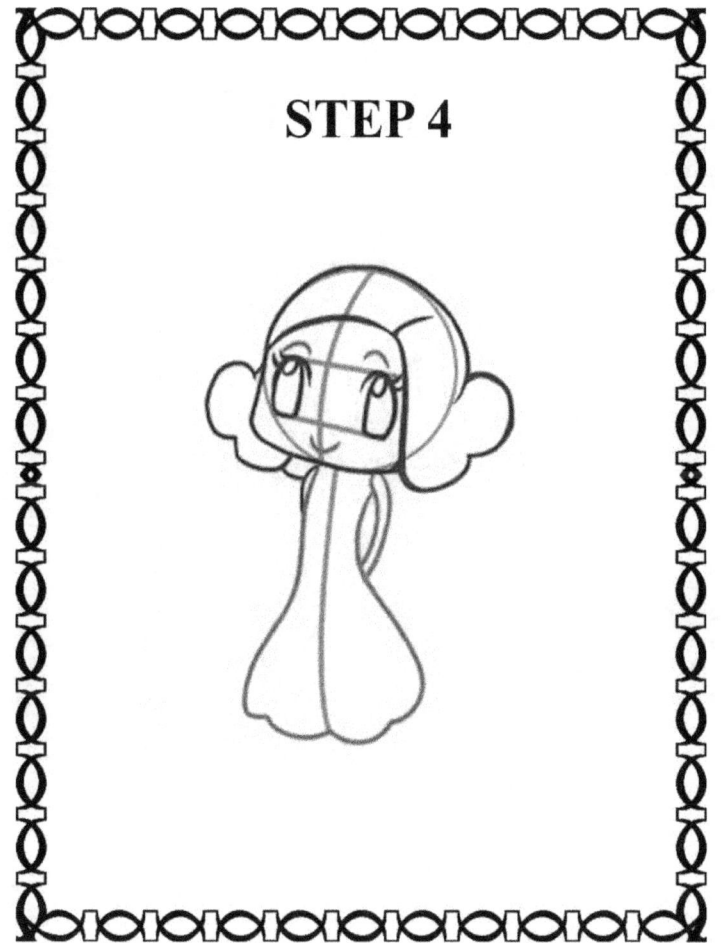

STEP 5

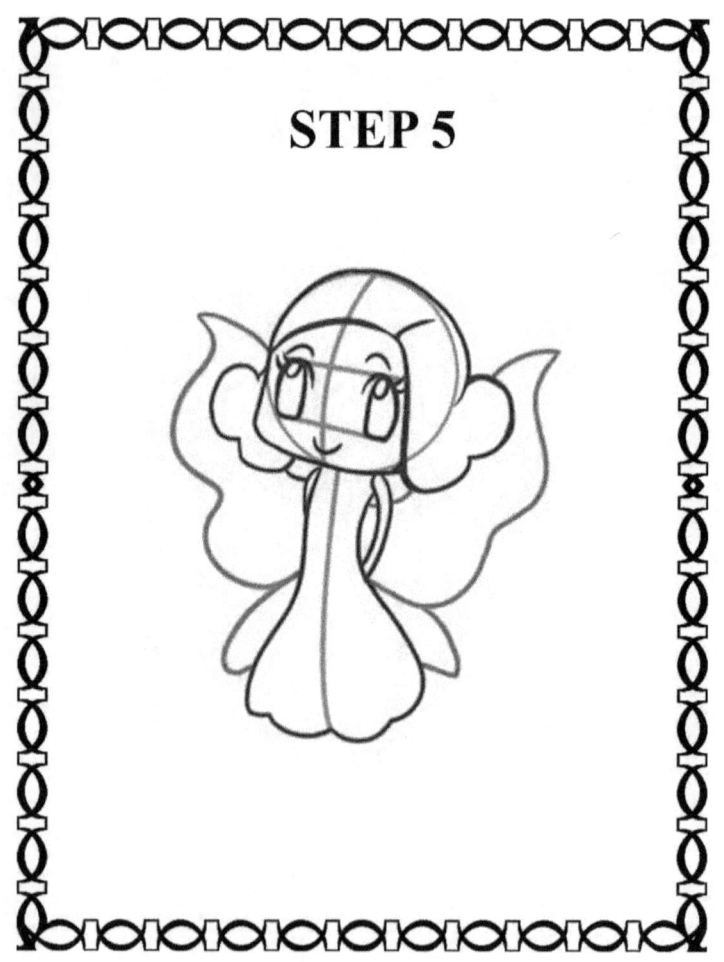

STEP 6

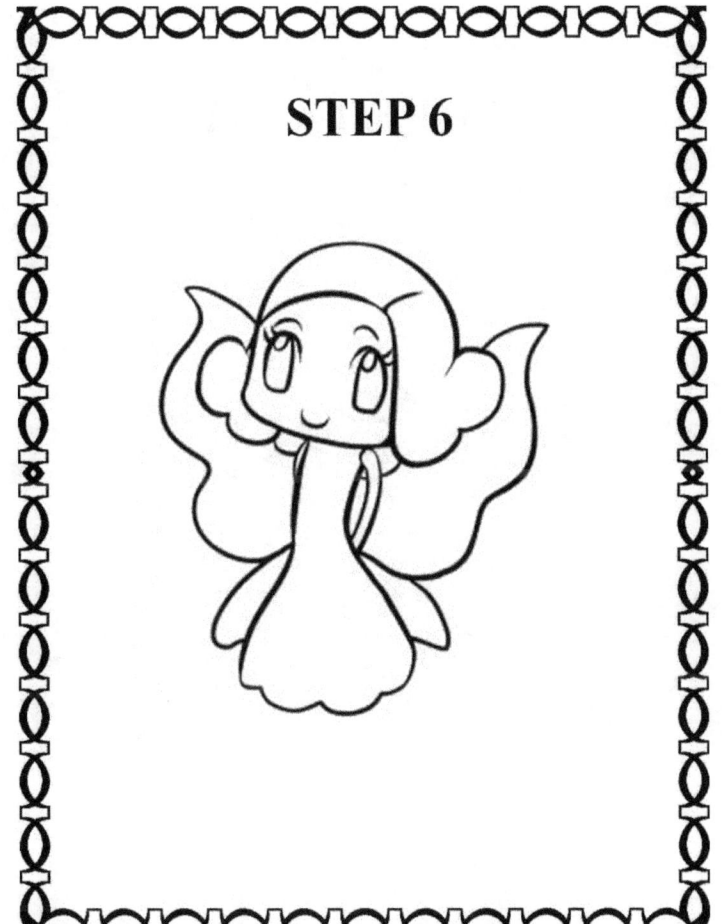

TREE FAIRY

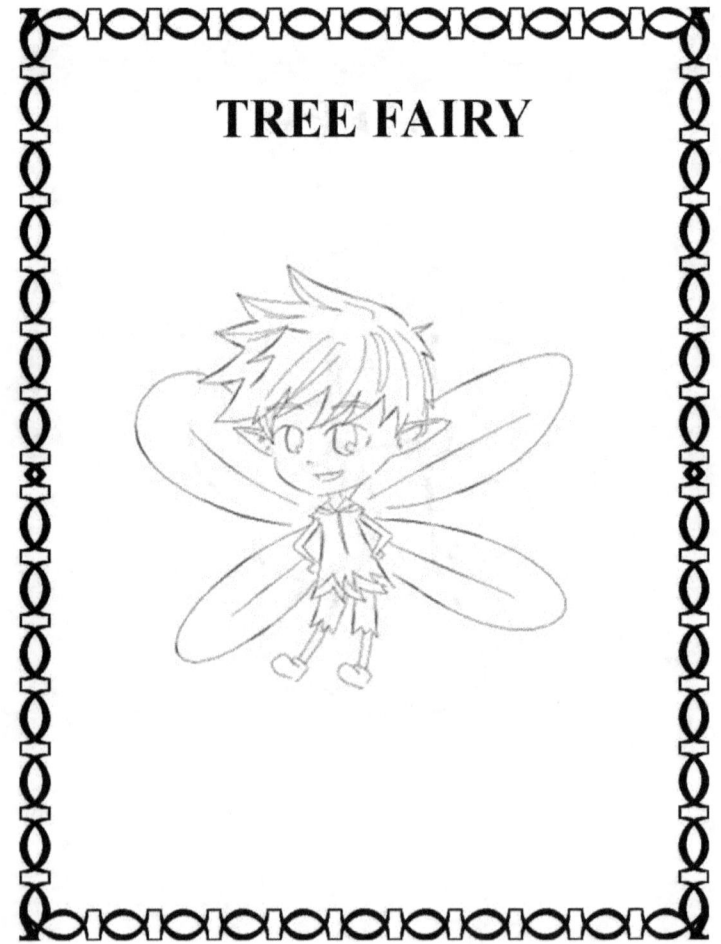

STEP 1

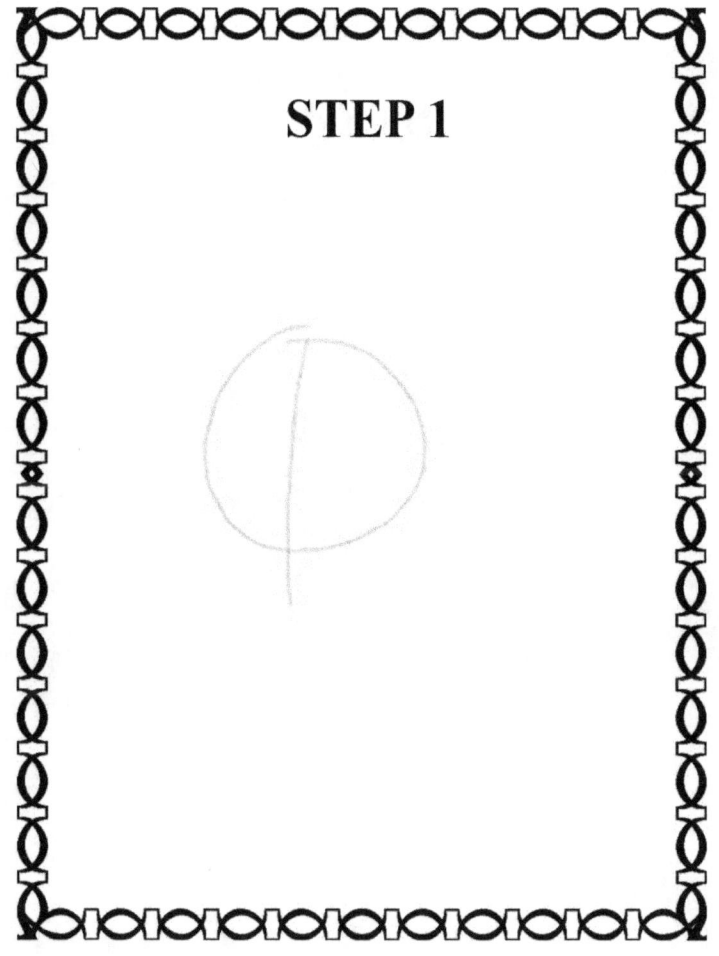

STEP 2

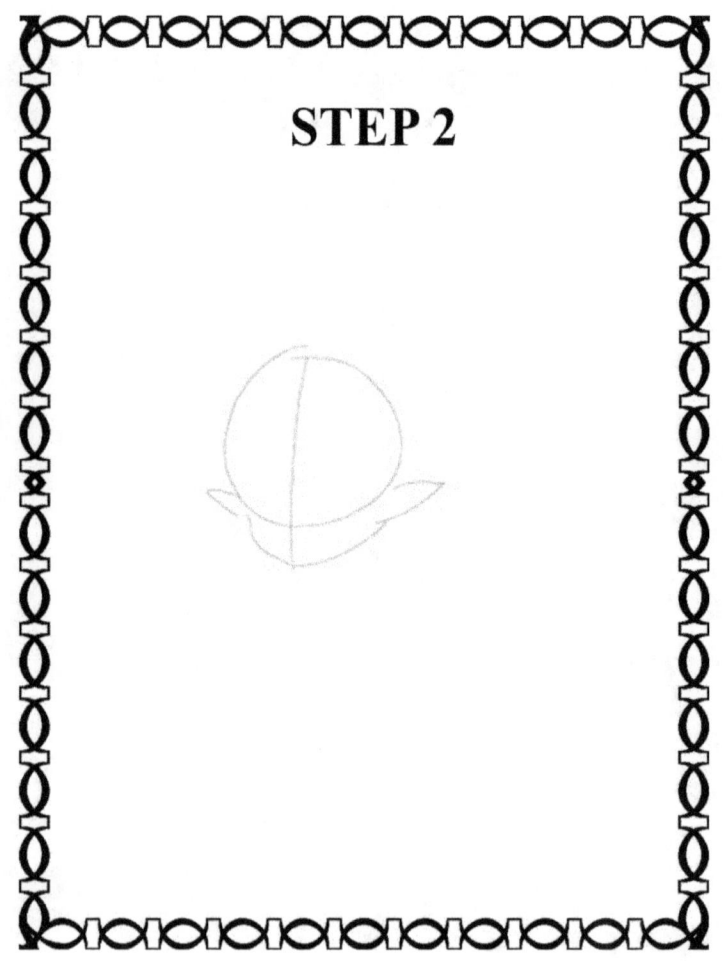

STEP 3

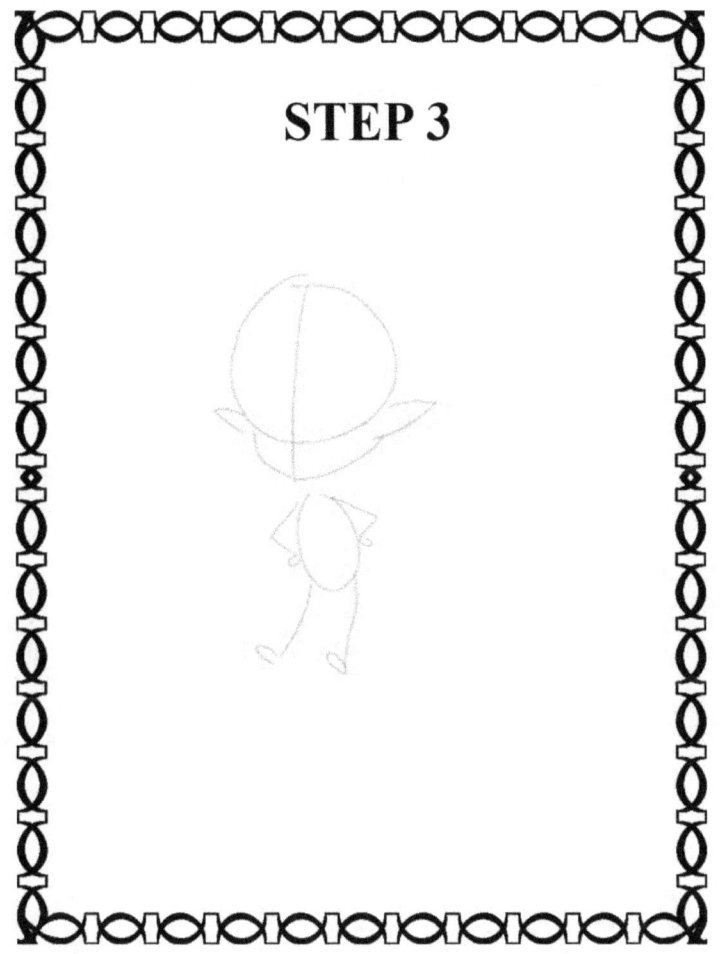

STEP 4

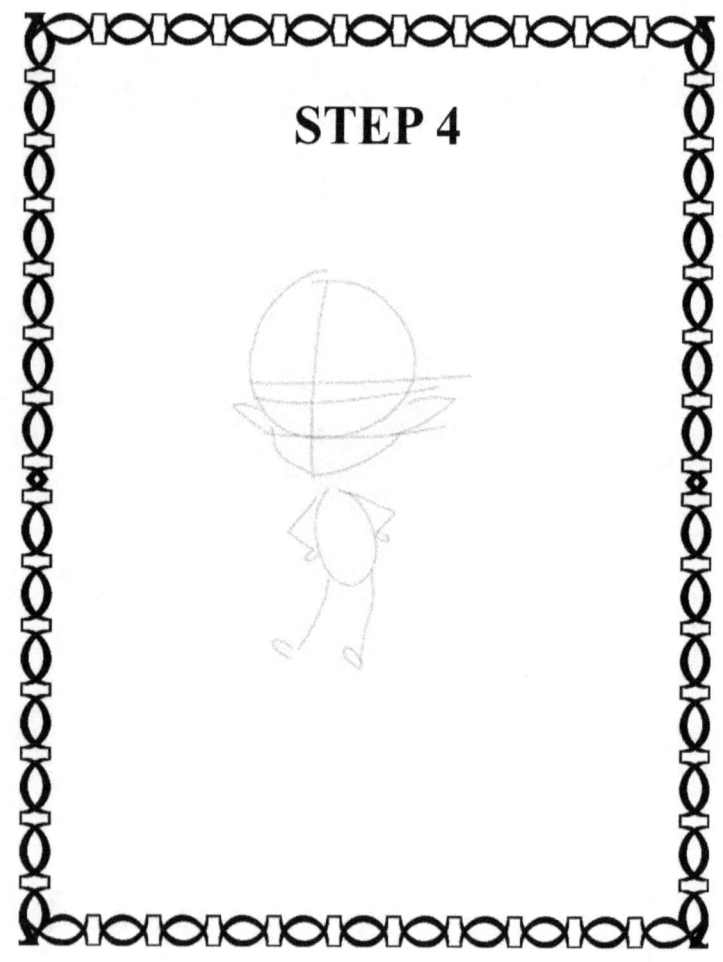

STEP 5

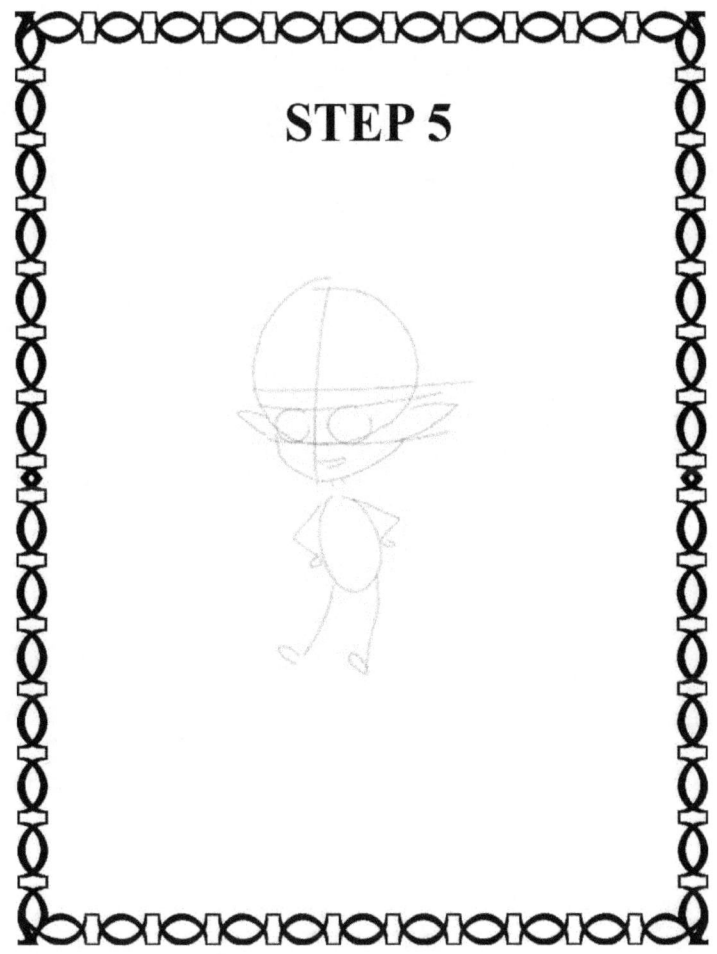

STEP 6

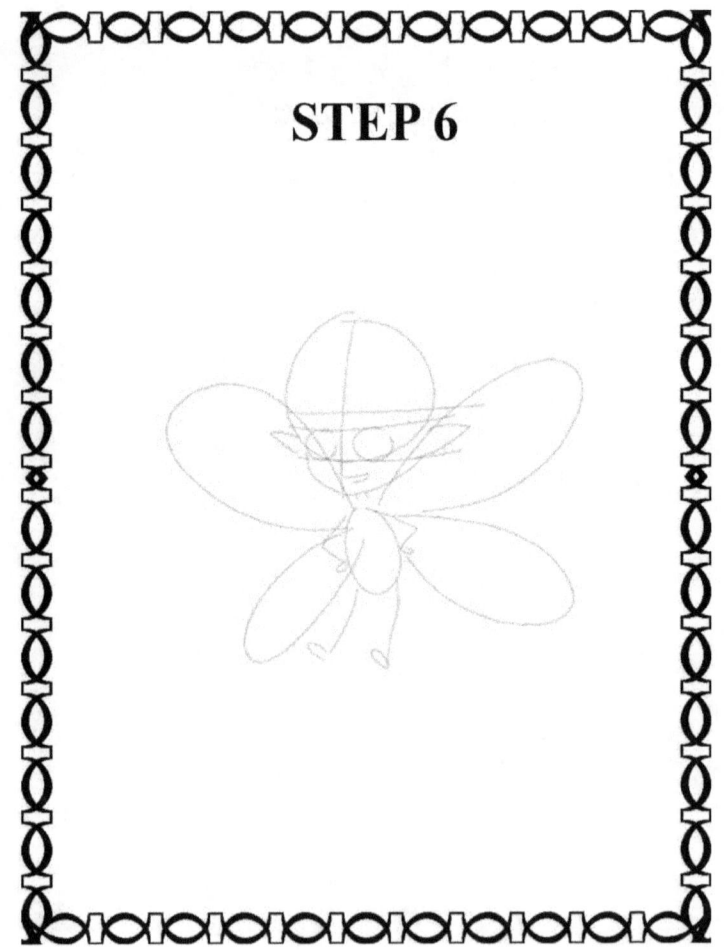

STEP 7

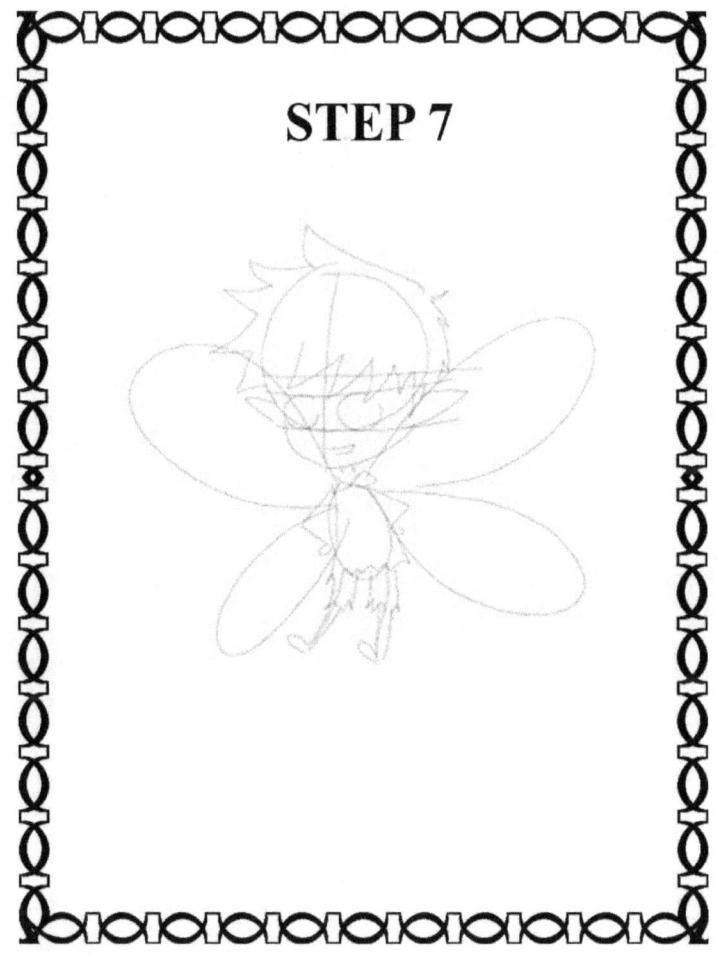

STEP 8

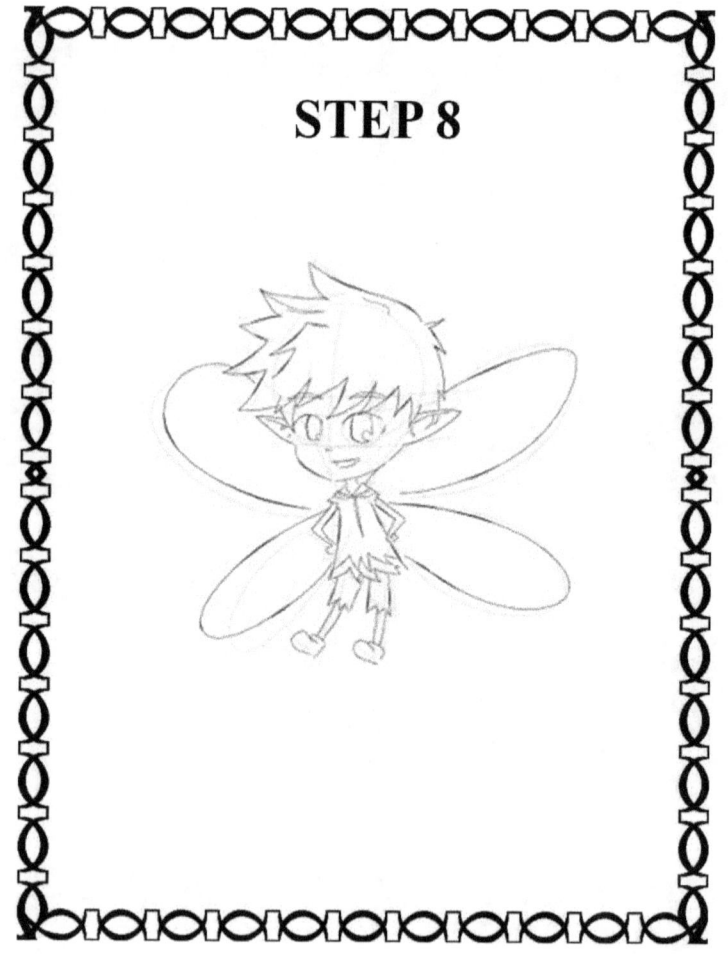

STEP 9

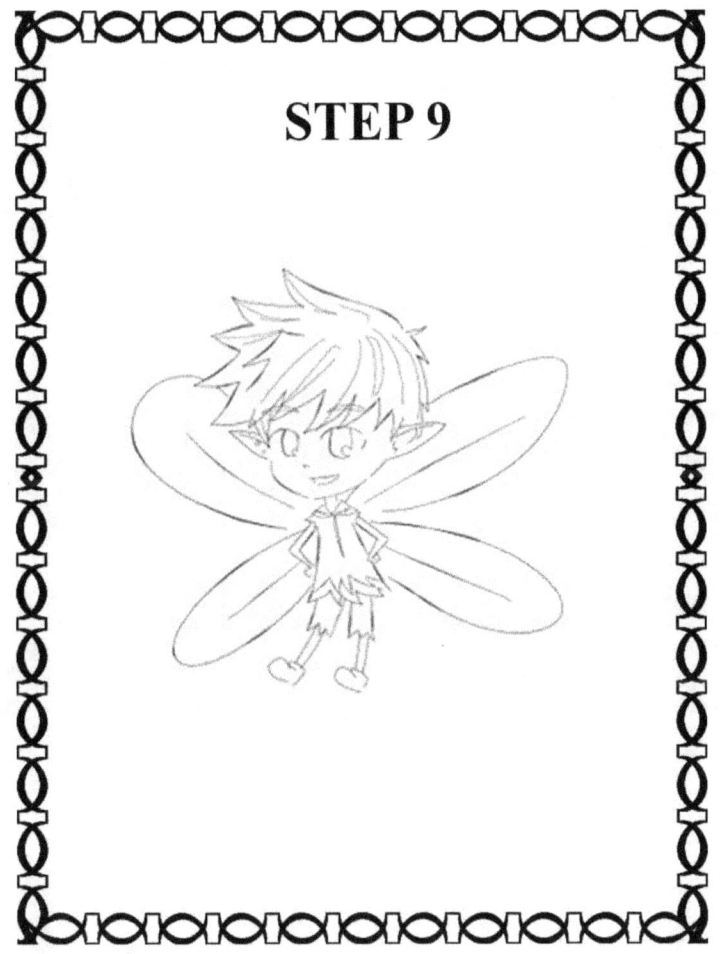